30 Minute Italian Meals Made Simple

LAMONA

Exclusive to Howdens Joinery Co.

HOWDENS

JOINERY CO.

MAKING SPACE MORE VALUABLE

Angela Boggiano

30 Minute Italian Meals Made Simple

As life gets busier, the quicker we can prepare tasty meals, the better. The great thing about Italian cooking is it's all about simple flavours and letting the ingredients speak for themselves – so with these recipes, you can rustle up all kinds of dishes in no time at all.

They're all designed to take no more than 30 minutes – and many of them a lot less. So whether you're cooking for the family or planning a dinner party, you'll find plenty of delicious, quick and easy meals.

All the recipes have been cooked using Lamona appliances, so you can be confident they'll turn out well. If you're a keen cook, there are interesting new dishes to try, as well as many Italian classics. And if you only cook now and again, this book will inspire you to get in the kitchen more often.

The Lamona range is all about great design, reliability and excellent value for money – and these Italian recipes are the ideal way to put the appliances through their paces.

Angela Boggiano
Food Writer and Home Economist

The Italian Kitchen

Famous for creating exceptionally stylish interiors, Italian designers have a huge influence on Howdens kitchens. The Italian kitchen is the perfect place for anyone who loves to cook, combining great design and functionality. The kitchen shown and a number of the products featured are produced in Italy and take inspiration from Italian design.

Our Italian Connection

We source a selection of Howdens products from Italy, including our Tewkesbury and Burford kitchens. One of the suppliers of these kitchens, ILCAM, is based in Fruili, North East Italy and was founded by Tullio Zamò in 1959.

Branching out from kitchen manufacturing in 1978, Tullio acquired five hectares of vineyards on the slopes of Rocca Bernarda. He began to expand the family business, Le Vigne di Zamò (the wine of Zamò), an inn established by his father many years before.

The Zamò family, led by Tullio's sons Silvano and Pierluigi, now manage 55 hectares of vineyards and produce numerous award-winning wines. The Gambero Rosso / Slow Food Italian Wines Guide awarded Three Glasses (which indicates an "extraordinary wine") to 12 of its wines, including the 1988, 1990, 1992 and 1994 vintages of Ronco dei Roseti.

www.levignedizamo.com

Vineyard managed by the Zamò family

Griddled Tuna with Fennel, Lemon and Mint Salad

Pinot Grigio and Ronco dei Roseti

Silvano, Brigitte and Pierluigi Zamò

Antipasti / Starters

Literally 'before the meal', antipasti can be small, light bites or more substantial starters – hot or cold. Here I've collected a range of ideas, capturing a variety of authentic Italian flavours. All quick and simple to prepare, and all extremely tempting.

Tomato, Basil and Ricotta Bruschetta

Tomato, Basil and Ricotta Bruschetta

Bruschetta is a classic Italian appetiser, and goes wonderfully with pre-dinner drinks. The creamy ricotta and the basil dressing are light yet really tasty – perfect to whet your appetite.

Serves 4 15 mins preparation, 5 mins cooking

Ingredients
1 small olive ciabatta loaf, cut into 12 x 1cm slices
1 small garlic clove
25g basil leaves, plus extra for garnish
1 tablespoon flaked almonds, toasted
2 tablespoons olive oil
Juice of ½ lemon
Sea salt and milled black pepper
250g ricotta cheese
200g vine ripened tomatoes, roughly chopped

Griddle pan
Food processor or pestle and mortar

1. Heat a griddle pan until it's very hot, and toast the ciabatta slices on both sides until they're nicely browned.

2. Place the garlic, basil and flaked almonds in a food processor, and whiz until you have a coarse paste. Or you can pound them in a pestle and mortar.

3. Add the olive oil and lemon juice, and whiz or pound again, adding enough water to make a pourable dressing. Season to taste with salt and plenty of pepper.

4. Spread the ricotta over the toasted ciabatta slices, and top with the chopped tomatoes. Drizzle the basil dressing over, and scatter with basil leaves to serve.

Broad Bean, Mint and Lemon Salad

Broad Bean, Mint and Lemon Salad

This fresh-tasting salad is best during the summer, when broad beans are in season – but if you can't get them, frozen beans are a good substitute. Either way, the mint enhances the freshness of the beans, and the saltiness of the pancetta balances all the flavours beautifully.

Serves 4 15 mins preparation, 5 mins cooking

Ingredients
8 thin slices pancetta
350g freshly shelled or frozen broad beans
1 garlic clove
2 tablespoons extra virgin olive oil, plus extra for drizzling
Juice and grated zest of ½ lemon
Sea salt and milled black pepper
1 large handful fresh mint, chopped
4 slices sourdough bread

1. Pre-heat the grill to high.

2. Lay the pancetta on a rack inside the grill tray. Grill for 4-5 minutes, until lightly golden and crisp. Put to one side to cool.

3. Bring a large pan of salted water to the boil. Add the beans and cook for 2-3 minutes if they're fresh, or 4 minutes if they're frozen – they should be just tender.

4. Drain the beans well, refresh them in cold water, and drain again.

5. To make the dressing, crush half the garlic clove. Place it in a small bowl, and whisk together with the extra virgin olive oil, lemon juice and zest, a pinch of salt and plenty of pepper.

6. To serve, drizzle the dressing over the beans, add the mint, and gently toss together. Toast the sourdough slices, then rub the remaining garlic over them and drizzle with a little oil. Place one slice of bread on each of 4 serving plates and pile the beans on top. Add 2 pancetta slices to each one, and serve immediately.

Fresh Anchovy Fritto Misto

Fresh anchovies have a deliciously mild, fresh flavour compared to the salted, canned variety. They're amazing served like this, quickly fried and piping hot for a real taste of the Mediterranean. Traditionally, small fresh anchovies can be eaten whole, but ask your fishmonger to gut and debone any larger ones.

Serves 4 10 mins preparation, 5 mins cooking

Ingredients
400g fresh anchovies
1 lemon
3 tablespoons flat-leaf parsley, very finely chopped
50g plain flour
50g cornflour
50g fine polenta
1 pinch cayenne pepper
Sea salt and milled black pepper
1 litre olive oil

Large baking tray
Fryer or large pan

1. Pre-heat the oven to 150°C/fan 130°C/gas mark 2.

2. Line a large baking tray with plenty of kitchen paper.

3. Place the anchovies in a shallow dish. Squeeze over the juice of half a lemon, and sprinkle with 2 tablespoons of the chopped parsley.

4. In another shallow dish, mix together the flour, cornflour, polenta and cayenne pepper. Season well with a pinch of salt and plenty of pepper.

5. In an electric deep fryer or large pan, heat the olive oil to 190°C. (To test the temperature, put a cube of bread in the pan. At 190°C, it will brown in 30 seconds.)

6. Coat the anchovies in the flour mixture, and shake off any excess. In small batches, place in the hot oil and fry for 1 minute, until crisp and lightly golden.

7. Use a slotted spoon to lift the anchovies onto the paper-lined baking tray. Keep warm in the oven while you prepare and cook the rest.

8. Serve scattered with the remaining parsley and wedges of lemon.

Fresh Anchovy Fritto Misto

Roasted Pepper, Taleggio and Sun-Blushed Tomato Frittata

Roasted Pepper, Taleggio and Sun-Blushed Tomato Frittata

Taleggio is a creamy, flavourful cheese that melts beautifully into this frittata – an Italian-style omelette, best enjoyed at room temperature. Served with salad leaves this makes a lovely, satisfying starter.

Serves 6 10 mins preparation, 20 mins cooking

Ingredients
400g new potatoes
6 large free range eggs, lightly beaten
200g jar roasted red peppers, drained and sliced into strips
150g Taleggio cheese, rind removed and cubed
1 large handful fresh basil
100g sun-blushed tomatoes, halved
2 tablespoons extra virgin olive oil

To serve
50g rocket leaves
Juice of ½ lemon
Sea salt

23cm ovenproof non-stick frying pan (without a plastic handle)

1. Place the potatoes in a medium saucepan and cover with water. Bring to the boil and cook for 7 minutes until tender. Drain and let them cool.

2. When the potatoes are cool enough to handle, use a sharp knife to cut into slices, about the thickness of a pound coin.

3. Add the beaten eggs to the potatoes, along with the strips of pepper, cubes of cheese, most of the basil, and the tomatoes. Gently fold everything together.

4. Pre-heat the grill to medium.

5. Heat half the extra virgin olive oil over a low heat in a 23cm non-stick frying pan, and gently tip in the egg mixture. Cook very gently for 10-12 minutes, until nearly set.

6. Place the frying pan under the grill to finish cooking for a further 3-4 minutes, until the frittata is set and golden.

7. Place the rocket leaves and remaining basil in a bowl, and toss with the lemon juice, remaining extra virgin olive oil and a pinch of salt.

8. Cut the frittata into wedges, and serve with the rocket and basil salad.

Ricotta Cakes with Mixed Tomato Salad

These lovely, light 'cakes' make a refreshing yet satisfying starter, served with the season's best tomatoes in a simple basil dressing.

Serves 4 15 mins preparation, 5 mins cooking

Ingredients
250g ricotta cheese
3 tablespoons Parmesan cheese, finely grated, plus extra for serving
3 tablespoons plain flour
Sea salt
1 large egg, lightly beaten
Zest of ½ lemon, finely grated
Milled black pepper
300g mixed tomatoes, such as cherry, vine or plum
1 handful fresh basil, roughly chopped
2 teaspoons balsamic vinegar
2 tablespoons extra virgin olive oil
1 tablespoon olive oil

1. Place the ricotta in a bowl with the Parmesan, flour, a pinch of salt, egg and lemon zest. Add a good grinding of pepper, and mix well. Put the mixture in the fridge for 5 minutes to firm up.

2. Place the mixed tomatoes in a bowl, cutting the large ones into pieces. Toss with the basil, balsamic vinegar and extra virgin olive oil. Season with salt and pepper to taste.

3. Heat the olive oil in a non-stick frying pan, and place tablespoons of the cheese mixture in the pan – you should have enough to make 12 ricotta cakes.

4. Cook the cakes for a few minutes until golden, then turn with a palette knife and cook on the other side.

5. Serve at once with a sprinkling of extra Parmesan and the tomato salad.

Ricotta Cakes with Mixed Tomato Salad

Deep-Fried Bocconcini with Salad

Bocconcini are small balls of mozzarella. Here, they have a crispy breadcrumb coating and a soft, melting centre – and we serve them alongside tasty leaves with a sweet balsamic dressing.

Serves 4 10 mins preparation, 15 mins cooking

Ingredients
100g stale white breadcrumbs
Grated zest of 1 small lemon
1 small handful fresh thyme leaves
Sea salt and milled black pepper
50g plain flour
2 large free range eggs, beaten
150g Bocconcini mozzarella balls, drained
Vegetable oil for frying
100g mixed radicchio, chicory and rocket leaves
2 teaspoons balsamic vinegar
2 tablespoons extra virgin olive oil

1. In a medium bowl, mix the breadcrumbs, lemon zest and thyme, and season with salt and pepper.

2. Place the flour in a second bowl and the eggs in a third.

3. Pat the mozzarella balls dry with kitchen paper. Roll them in the flour, then dip in the egg before rolling in the breadcrumb mixture. Repeat this, to create a double layer of egg and breadcrumbs on the outside of the mozzarella balls.

4. Half fill a saucepan with vegetable oil. Heat over a high heat to 190°C. (To test the temperature, put a cube of bread in the pan. At 190°C, it will brown in 30 seconds.)

5. Using a slotted spoon, lower the crumbed mozzarella balls, a few at a time, into the hot oil. Fry for 2-3 minutes until golden brown, then remove from the oil and drain on kitchen paper.

6. Place the salad leaves in a large bowl, and toss with the balsamic vinegar and extra virgin olive oil. Serve together with the Bocconcini.

Deep-Fried Bocconcini with Salad

24

Primi Piatti / First Courses

You've probably noticed how Italian menus don't really count antipasti as a course, so what follows is called the 'first course'. This is often pasta, risotto or sometimes soup. In this section, I've included recipes for all of these, giving you plenty to choose from when you're planning an Italian meal.

Soups

Italian soups tend to be more substantial than British ones, and usually include pasta or beans. So they're an important part of a meal, or even a meal in themselves. These recipes show just how satisfying they can be – and, of course, how tasty.

Tortellini in Brodo

Tortellini in Brodo

Brodo traditionally refers to a thin soup of meat, fish or vegetable stock. This wonderfully restorative chicken soup uses small filled tortellini – but you could use small pasta shapes, or even spaghetti broken into small pieces instead. The final grating of Parmesan is very important!

Serves 4 5 mins preparation, 25 mins cooking

Ingredients
900ml fresh, well-flavoured chicken stock
1 large chicken leg, including the thigh, skin removed
1 carrot, peeled and chopped
1 celery stick, chopped
1 onion, halved and chopped
1 bay leaf
6 peppercorns
1 small bunch flat-leaf parsley
100g small filled tortellini or cappelletti
4 tablespoons Parmesan cheese, grated

1. Pour the chicken stock into a saucepan, and add the chicken leg, carrot, celery, onion, bay leaf, peppercorns and parsley. Bring to a gentle simmer, and cook for 15-20 minutes until the chicken is cooked through.

2. Remove the chicken from the pan and put to one side to cool slightly. When cool enough to handle, remove the meat from the bone and chop into pieces.

3. Strain the stock into a clean saucepan. Bring to the boil, and add the tortellini or cappelletti, and simmer for a few minutes.

4. Add the chopped chicken and the chopped carrot from the stock, and serve with grated Parmesan.

Winter Vegetable Minestrone Soup

Winter Vegetable Minestrone Soup

There's no comparison between shop-bought minestrone and this hearty homemade version. And the last-minute addition of pesto sauce makes even more of a delicious difference.

Serves 4 10 mins preparation, 20 mins cooking

Ingredients
1 tablespoon olive oil
1 small onion, finely chopped
2 garlic cloves, finely chopped
1 large leek, finely chopped
2 medium potatoes, peeled and diced
1 large carrot, peeled and diced
1 sprig rosemary, leaves finely chopped
400g tinned chopped tomatoes
400ml vegetable stock
100g small pasta shapes
75g Savoy cabbage, finely shredded
400g tinned borlotti or cannellini beans

To serve
2 teaspoons basil pesto
3 tablespoons Parmesan cheese, grated
Sourdough bread, sliced and toasted

1. Heat the olive oil in a large saucepan, and add the onion and garlic. Cook for 2 minutes, then stir in the leek, potatoes, carrot and rosemary, and cook for another 5 minutes.

2. Tip in the chopped tomatoes, and pour in the vegetable stock. Bring to a simmer, and cook for a further 10 minutes.

3. Meanwhile, bring a small saucepan of water to the boil, and cook the pasta for 4 minutes until 'al dente' (firm but not hard). Drain it well.

4. Stir the cabbage into the soup, and cook for 3 minutes before stirring in the pasta and beans. Heat these through for just a few minutes.

5. Ladle the soup into bowls, and serve with a dollop of pesto and a sprinkling of Parmesan. Toasted sourdough is a nice accompaniment.

Cannellini Bean and Cavolo Nero Soup

If you've not tried it before, cavolo nero is a very tasty Italian cabbage with dark green leaves – and this soup is incredibly simple to make, but absolutely packed full of flavour. Adding stale bread may seem strange, but it thickens the broth and gives a lovely silky texture.

Serves 4 5 mins preparation, 25 mins cooking

Ingredients
2 tablespoons olive oil
1 large onion, finely chopped
100g cubed pancetta
2 garlic cloves, finely chopped
1 sprig rosemary, finely chopped
1 pinch chilli flakes (optional)
400g tinned plum tomatoes
1 litre vegetable stock
200g cavolo nero, finely chopped
400g tinned cannellini beans
35g stale bread, broken into small pieces

To serve
Extra virgin olive oil

1. Heat the olive oil in a large saucepan, and cook the onion gently for about 6 minutes. Add the pancetta, and continue cooking for 4 minutes.

2. Add the garlic, rosemary and chilli flakes (if you're using them). Cook for a minute, then add the plum tomatoes and vegetable stock.

3. Stir in the cavolo nero, beans and bread. Let the cavolo nero wilt down, and then cook for another 10 minutes.

4. Serve the soup drizzled with a really good peppery extra virgin olive oil.

Cannellini Bean and Cavolo Nero Soup

Pasta and Risotto

When we think of Italian food, most of us think of pasta. You probably have a favourite dish, but I hope these recipes will tempt you to try something different – perhaps a less common pasta shape like Trofie, or a distinctive regional sauce, such as 'alla Norma'. I've also included a delicious risotto, using classic Italian ingredients.

Tagliolini Alla Norma

Tagliolini Alla Norma

You'll find this recipe all over the island of Sicily, where aubergines grow in abundance. They make a rich vegetarian sauce, which lends itself well to a generous grating of creamy Pecorino cheese.

Serves 4 10 mins preparation, 20 mins cooking

Ingredients
2 tablespoons olive oil
1 large aubergine, diced
2 shallots, finely chopped
2 garlic cloves, finely chopped
1 red chilli, finely chopped
1 pinch dried oregano
400g fresh tomatoes, roughly chopped, or
400g tinned chopped tomatoes
1 tablespoon balsamic vinegar
200ml water
400g dried tagliolini pasta
1 small bunch fresh basil, roughly chopped
50g fresh young Pecorino cheese shavings

1. Heat the olive oil in a large saucepan, and fry the aubergine for 5 minutes until it starts to brown and soften.

2. Add the shallots, garlic, chilli and oregano, and cook for a few minutes more.

3. Stir in the tomatoes and balsamic vinegar, and 200ml of water. Simmer gently for 15 minutes – until the tomatoes are really soft, and the sauce is reduced and thickened.

4. While the sauce is cooking, bring a large pan of water to the boil and cook the tagliolini according to the packet instructions.

5. Drain the pasta and return to the pan. Add the sauce and chopped basil, and toss well into the pasta. Serve with the Pecorino shavings.

Ligurian Trofie Pasta with Green Beans, Potato and Pesto

Trofie are short, thin, knotted strips of pasta, from Liguria in north-western Italy.
The region is also famous for its fresh basil, so pesto sauce is Trofie's perfect partner.
Of course, you can buy decent ready-made pesto but making your own is pretty easy,
and gives the finished dish extra depth of flavour.

Serves 4 5 mins preparation, 15-20 mins cooking

Ingredients

350g Trofie pasta or any short pasta
250g small new potatoes, halved
100g fine green beans

4 tablespoons basil pesto sauce (see below)
4 tablespoons Parmesan cheese, finely grated

1. Bring a large pan of water to the boil. Add the pasta and cook for 5 minutes, until it starts to soften.

2. Add the new potatoes and cook for 5 minutes more, then add the green beans and cook for a final 3-4 minutes until tender.

3. Drain the pasta, potatoes and beans, saving a ladleful of the cooking water, and return to the pan.

4. Add the pesto sauce and a little of the cooking water. Stir well, then sprinkle with the Parmesan and serve immediately.

Basil Pesto Sauce

Serves 4 10 mins preparation

Ingredients

1 small garlic clove
1 pinch sea salt
25g pine nuts, very lightly toasted
50g fresh basil

25g Parmesan cheese, finely grated
Juice of ½ lemon
75ml extra virgin olive oil

1. Place the garlic in a pestle and mortar with the sea salt, and pound until you've crushed the garlic to a paste. Add the pine nuts and basil, and continue to pound until you have a coarse paste. (If you prefer, you can do this stage in a food processor.)

2. Transfer the paste to a bowl, and stir in the Parmesan, lemon juice and extra virgin olive oil – along with enough water to make a thick sauce.

   Fresh pesto can be made in advance and stored in the fridge in a sealed container with a thin layer of olive oil on the top for up to 5 days.

Ligurian Trofie Pasta with Green Beans, Potato and Pesto

Pappardelle with Fennel and Italian Sausage Ragu

Pappardelle is the lovely wide ribbon pasta that goes brilliantly with chunky, meaty sauces. For this one, try to get hold of really good Italian sausages, as they make all the difference to the taste and texture.

Serves 4 5 mins preparation, 25 mins cooking

Ingredients
2 tablespoons olive oil
1 small onion, finely chopped
2 garlic cloves, finely chopped
2 teaspoons fennel seeds
1 sprig rosemary, leaves finely chopped
400g good quality Italian sausages
1 tablespoon tomato purée
400g tinned chopped tomatoes
Sea salt and milled black pepper
400g fresh pappardelle pasta

To serve
4 tablespoons Parmesan cheese, grated
1 small bunch flat-leaf parsley, finely chopped

1. Heat the oil in a large, heavy-based frying pan, and fry the onion for 5 minutes until it begins to soften.

2. Stir in the garlic, fennel seeds and rosemary, and cook for a further minute.

3. Split open the sausages and add the meat to the pan. Fry gently, breaking up the meat with a wooden spoon.

4. Add the tomato purée, and cook with the sausages for a minute before tipping in the chopped tomatoes.

5. Season the sauce with a pinch of salt and a good grinding of pepper, and simmer for 10-15 minutes until thickened.

6. While the sauce is simmering, bring a large pan of water to the boil and cook the pappardelle for a few minutes – until tender but still firm. Drain it well, saving a ladleful of the cooking water, and return it to the pan.

7. Ladle the sauce into the pan with the pasta, adding the cooking water you've saved. Toss everything together gently, and pile it into bowls, sprinkling with Parmesan and chopped flat-leaf parsley.

Pappardelle with Fennel and Italian Sausage Ragu

Fresh Pesto Lasagne

Fresh Pesto Lasagne

Although traditionally served as a first course in Italy, this simple, meat-free lasagne makes a lovely light lunch or supper – and using homemade pesto adds the vibrant taste of fresh basil.

Serves 4-6 10 mins preparation, 20 mins cooking

Ingredients
100g fresh pesto (see page 38 for my recipe)
250g fresh lasagne sheets
250ml mascarpone
250g mozzarella, drained and roughly grated
4 tablespoons Parmesan cheese, finely grated

To serve
2 tablespoons pine nuts, lightly toasted
1 small handful basil leaves

1 litre ovenproof dish

1. Pre-heat the oven to 180°C/fan 160°C/gas mark 4.

2. Spread 2 tablespoons of pesto over the base of a deep, 1 litre ovenproof dish. Place a large sheet of lasagne on top, and then spread this with a little more pesto.

3. Dot teaspoons of mascarpone on top, and scatter over a quarter of the mozzarella.

4. Place another sheet of lasagne on top, and repeat the layers as above, finishing with a top layer of mascarpone and mozzarella.

5. Sprinkle the Parmesan over the lasagne, and bake for 15-20 minutes until it's cooked through and bubbling.

6. To serve, sprinkle with toasted pine nuts and basil leaves.

Vongole Linguine

Vongole Linguine

This classic dish of clams and pasta is extremely popular in many parts of Italy. For me, what makes it is the garlicky white-wine broth you get, with just a hint of the taste of the sea.

Serves 4 15 mins preparation, 15 mins cooking

Ingredients
1kg small clams, scrubbed clean
400g linguine pasta
2 tablespoons extra virgin olive oil
4 garlic cloves, finely sliced
1 large bunch flat-leaf parsley, stalks finely chopped and leaves roughly chopped
Sea salt and milled black pepper
250ml white wine
Grated zest of 1 lemon
1 pinch chilli flakes (optional)

To serve
Crusty bread

1. Sort through the cleaned clams. If any aren't tightly closed, give them a tap – if they don't close, throw them away.

2. Bring a large pan of water to the boil, and cook the linguine according to the packet instructions.

3. Meanwhile, in another large saucepan, heat the extra virgin olive oil gently. Add the garlic, and cook for 30 seconds until it starts turning a golden colour.

4. Add the flat-leaf parsley stalks and a pinch of salt and pepper, then add the white wine and clams. Give everything a good shake, and put the lid on the pan.

5. After about 3-4 minutes, the clams will start to open. Keep shaking the pan until they've all opened.

6. Drain the pasta, and add it to the pan of clams, along with the lemon zest, chilli flakes (if you're using them), and the chopped parsley leaves.

7. Toss together well, and serve with crusty bread to mop up the delicious juices.

Spaghetti with Broad Beans, Tomatoes and Creamy Goats' Cheese

Spaghetti with Broad Beans, Tomatoes and Creamy Goats' Cheese

Enjoy this light, fresh-flavoured pasta dish in the summer, when broad beans are in season. It takes hardly any cooking, so it's great for a quick (but quite special) lunch.

Serves 4 10 mins preparation, 15 mins cooking

Ingredients
200g fresh broad beans (shelled weight)
2 tablespoons extra virgin olive oil
300g cherry tomatoes, quartered
2 garlic cloves, finely chopped
400g spaghetti
200g fresh baby spinach leaves
100g fresh mild goats' cheese, chopped

1. Bring a medium pan of water to the boil, and blanch the broad beans for a minute. Drain well and run under cold water. Remove the outer skins to reveal the bright green flesh.

2. Heat the extra virgin olive oil in a saucepan, and add the cherry tomatoes and garlic. Cook until the tomatoes are really soft and the garlic is lightly golden. Take the pan off the heat.

3. Bring a large pan of water to the boil, and cook the spaghetti according to the packet instructions. Drain and return it to the pan.

4. While the pasta is still hot, quickly add the tomatoes and garlic, spinach, broad beans and goats' cheese. Toss together gently, and serve immediately with a drizzle of extra virgin olive oil.

Pennette with Peas, Pancetta and Mascarpone

Pennette with Peas, Pancetta and Mascarpone

Slightly shorter and thinner than penne pasta, pennette is just the right shape to hold thick, creamy sauces – like the super-tasty one in this recipe. If you can't find pennette, penne will do the job too.

Serves 4 5 mins preparation, 15-20 mins cooking

Ingredients
400g pennette or penne pasta
2 tablespoons olive oil
1 small onion, finely chopped
150g cubed smoked pancetta
2 garlic cloves, finely chopped
200g frozen peas
200ml vegetable stock
125g mascarpone
1 small bunch fresh mint, finely chopped
Grated zest of 1 lemon
Sea salt and milled black pepper

1. Bring a large pan of water to the boil, and cook the pasta according to the packet instructions.

2. Meanwhile, heat the olive oil in a saucepan, and fry the onion for 5 minutes until it starts to soften.

3. Add the pancetta, and cook for another 5 minutes until golden.

4. Stir in the garlic and cook for a minute, then add the peas, vegetable stock and mascarpone, and simmer for a few more minutes.

5. Drain the pasta and return it to the pan, then add the creamy pancetta and peas, toss together well.

6. Stir in the mint and lemon zest, and season with a pinch of salt and plenty of pepper. Serve immediately.

Porcini and Fontina Risotto

You can't beat a rich, creamy, cheesy risotto. Adding dried porcini mushrooms to this recipe really intensifies the flavour.

Serves 4 5 mins preparation, 25 mins cooking

Ingredients
25g dried porcini mushrooms
1 knob of butter
2 tablespoons olive oil
250g mixed mushrooms, including chestnut,
large flat and Portobello
3 shallots, finely chopped
1 garlic clove, finely chopped
A few sprigs fresh thyme, chopped
350g risotto rice
300ml white wine
1 litre hot vegetable stock
100g fontina cheese, diced
1 handful flat-leaf parsley, finely chopped

1. Place the dried porcini in a bowl, and pour boiling water over them. Leave to soak for about 10 minutes.

2. Meanwhile, heat the butter and 1 tablespoon of the olive oil in a saucepan, and fry the other mushrooms until golden. Remove from the pan, and keep to one side.

3. Add the remaining olive oil to the pan, and fry the shallots for a few minutes until they begin to soften. Add the garlic and thyme and cook for a minute longer.

4. Drain the porcini mushrooms and chop roughly. Add them to the pan with the shallots, and mix together well.

5. Stir in the rice, and add the wine. Let this bubble rapidly, until the rice has absorbed the wine – it will take about 2 minutes.

6. Gradually add the hot stock to the pan, a ladleful at a time, letting the rice absorb each ladleful before adding the next. Keep doing this until all the liquid is absorbed – this will be around 20 minutes.

7. Gently stir in the fried mushrooms, fontina and parsley, and cover the pan. Let the risotto sit for 3 minutes before ladling into serving bowls.

Porcini and Fontina Risotto

Secondi / Main Courses

As with all Italian cooking, there's a great diversity
in the types of main courses enjoyed up and down
the country. I've put together this selection to show
you the range of tastes and styles – from delicate
fish dishes to hearty meat recipes, and featuring some
typically Italian ways with herbs, spices and vegetables.

Meat

Here I've put traditional favourites alongside more modern recipes. They're all unmistakably Italian, with flavour combinations you just don't find anywhere else. Some are great for family meals, others will impress at dinner parties – but none involve spending hours in the kitchen.

LAMONA

T-bone Steak with Garlic and Parsley

Here's how to cook a superbly succulent, tasty steak. A perfect supper for two.

Serves 2 5 mins preparation, 25 mins cooking

Ingredients
1 x 450g T-bone steak
3 tablespoons extra virgin olive oil
Sea salt and milled black pepper
1 handful flat-leaf parsley, roughly chopped
2 garlic cloves, crushed
500g potatoes, diced
2 sprigs rosemary, roughly chopped

To serve
Salad
Rosemary potatoes

1. Pre-heat the oven to 200°C/fan 180°C/gas mark 6.

2. Put the steak on a plate, and rub with 2 tablespoons of the extra virgin olive oil and plenty of salt and pepper. Leave at room temperature for about 10 minutes.

3. Meanwhile, place the potatoes on a baking tray and toss with the rosemary and the remaining extra virgin olive oil. Place in the oven and roast for 20 minutes until golden and crunchy.

4. Heat a griddle pan until searingly hot. Add the meat with the oil from the plate, and sear for 3 minutes on the first side until well browned. Turn, and sear the other side for a further 3 minutes.

5. While this side is cooking, sprinkle the surface with half the parsley and garlic.

6. Transfer the steak to a small roasting tin, and sprinkle the other side with the remaining parsley and garlic. Place in the oven and roast for 15 minutes, turning half way through.

7. Leave the steak to rest for about 10 minutes, then slice and serve with salad leaves and roasted rosemary potatoes.

T-bone Steak with Garlic and Parsley

Pork Saltimbocca

Pork Saltimbocca

Meaning 'jumps in the mouth' in Italian, saltimbocca is a quick, simple classic dish, usually made with veal. This version with pork is just as good, and the thin escalopes cook in virtually no time at all.

Serves 4 5 mins preparation, 10 mins cooking

Ingredients
4 x 100g pork escalopes
4 slices Parma ham
4 sage leaves
2 tablespoons plain flour
2 tablespoons olive oil
1 knob of butter
100ml Marsala wine

To serve
Sauted potatoes
Wilted spinach

Cocktail sticks

1. Place the pork escalopes on a chopping board, and wrap a slice of Parma ham around each one. Attach a sage leaf to the pork and ham with a cocktail stick.

2. Put the plain flour in a shallow dish, and coat the pork escalopes lightly on both sides, shaking off any excess.

3. In a large frying pan, heat the olive oil over a medium heat. Then fry the escalopes for 3 minutes on each side, until cooked through.

4. Just towards the end of the cooking, increase the temperature. Add the butter and Marsala, and sizzle them in the pan for just a minute to make a sauce. Serve with sauted potatoes and wilted spinach.

Polpette with Roasted Squash and Sage

Polpette with Roasted Squash and Sage

These small, roasted meatballs are delicious cooked with sweet butternut squash and the earthy flavour of sage. Served with creamy mash or polenta, they make a really satisfying main course.

Serves 4 5 mins preparation, 25 mins cooking

Ingredients
250g minced pork
250g minced beef
100g stale breadcrumbs
1 large egg
50g Parmesan cheese, grated
4 tablespoons flat-leaf parsley, finely chopped
1 garlic clove, crushed
1 butternut squash, peeled and cut into wedges
1 small bunch sage leaves
1 tablespoon olive oil
250ml white wine

1. Pre-heat the oven to 200°C/fan 180°C/gas mark 6.

2. Place the pork, beef, breadcrumbs, egg, Parmesan, parsley and garlic in a large bowl, and mix together well. You may find it easier to use your hands for this.

3. Shape the mixture into 16 walnut-sized balls. Place the polpette in a non-stick roasting tin with the butternut squash and sage leaves. Drizzle over the olive oil, and toss together well.

4. Roast for 20 minutes, until the polpette are browned all over. Add the white wine and continue to cook for 5 minutes – the polpette should be cooked through, and the squash golden and tender.

Chicken and Olive Casserole

The combination of olives, tomatoes, capers and parsley is a winning formula with chicken. I like it best as a hearty supper dish, with rice or creamy polenta.

Serves 4 5 mins preparation, 25 mins cooking

Ingredients
2 tablespoons olive oil
1 large onion, finely chopped
2 garlic cloves, finely sliced
8 large boneless, skinless chicken thighs
1 large sprig rosemary, finely chopped
2 tablespoons sundried tomato paste
2 x 400g tinned chopped tomatoes
1 tablespoon runny honey
100g pitted green and black olives with herbs
2 tablespoons capers
1 small bunch flat-leaf parsley, roughly chopped,
plus extra for serving

Large casserole dish

To serve
Rice or polenta

1. Heat the olive oil in a large casserole dish on a medium heat. Add the onion and cook for a few minutes, before adding the garlic and cooking for a further minute. Remove the onion and garlic from the pan, and keep to one side on a plate.

2. Turn up the heat and add the chicken, cooking for a few minutes on each side until golden.

3. Return the onions and garlic to the casserole, and add all the remaining ingredients. Cover with a lid, and cook for 20 minutes until the chicken is cooked through – it should be juicy and tender, and the sauce rich and thick. Serve with rice or creamy polenta, scattered with extra chopped parsley.

Chicken and Olive Casserole

Lamb, Lemon and Red Onion Spiedini

Lamb, Lemon and Red Onion Spiedini

Lamb and anchovies may sound like an unusual pairing, but the flavours work brilliantly on these tasty skewers. In this recipe, I cooked them in a griddle pan, but they're also fantastic on the barbecue. I used long bay branches slightly sharpened at the ends as skewers.

Serves 2 15-20 mins preparation, 10 mins cooking

Ingredients
400g lamb fillet, cut into 1cm thick rounds
Juice of 1 lemon
3 tablespoons olive oil
2 anchovies in oil, mashed
1 garlic clove, crushed
3 tablespoons fresh thyme, chopped
1 lemon, thinly sliced
2 red onions, cut into wedges
10 bay leaves

Wooden or metal skewers
Griddle pan

1. Arrange the lamb rounds on a chopping board.

2. Place the lemon juice, olive oil, anchovies, garlic and thyme in a bowl, and mix together well. Brush this over the lamb.

3. Thread a slice of the lamb onto a wooden or metal skewer, followed by a slice of lemon, a wedge of onion and half a bay leaf. Repeat this 4 more times, so you have 5 pieces of everything on the skewer, and then fill 3 more skewers in the same way.

4. Heat a griddle pan until very hot. Sear the skewers for 5-6 minutes, turning a few times until the lamb is browned and cooked, basting with the olive oil and anchovy dressing as you go.

Chicken Escalopes with Lemon and Parmesan

Liven up chicken breasts with this crispy, zesty crumb coating. Then add a warm potato and red onion salad to make an impressive – yet very easy dish.

Serves 4 10 mins preparation, 20 mins cooking

Ingredients
4 skinless chicken breasts
150g fresh breadcrumbs
25g Parmesan cheese, finely grated
Grated zest of 1 lemon
1 large egg, beaten
3 tablespoons olive oil

To serve
400g new potatoes, halved or quartered, depending on their size
1 red onion, finely chopped
3 tablespoons flat-leaf parsley, finely chopped
2 tablespoons extra virgin olive oil
Rocket leaves

1. Place the chicken breasts between sheets of greaseproof paper, and place on a chopping board. Using a rolling pin, bash the chicken to flatten it, until 1cm thick.

2. Mix the breadcrumbs with the Parmesan and lemon zest, and place in a shallow dish. Place the beaten egg in a separate shallow dish.

3. Dip the chicken in the egg, and then into the breadcrumb mixture, pressing down well to coat evenly.

4. Heat the olive oil in a large non-stick frying pan. Fry the chicken for 4-5 minutes on each side over a medium heat, until cooked through and the coating is crunchy and golden.

5. While you're preparing the chicken, place the potatoes in a saucepan and cover with water. Bring to the boil and simmer for 12 minutes, until they're very tender.

6. Drain the potatoes, and return them to the pan. Toss with the red onion and flat-leaf parsley and a drizzle of extra virgin olive oil.

7. Serve the chicken with the potatoes and a handful of rocket.

Chicken Escalopes with Lemon and Parmesan

Steak Pizzaiola

Steak Pizzaiola

The secret of this simple steak dish is to have tasty tomatoes and fresh oregano for the Pizzaiola sauce – so it's a great one to do in late summer, when tomatoes are ripe and plentiful.

Serves 2 5 mins preparation, 15 mins cooking

Ingredients
2 tablespoons olive oil
2 x 300g rump steaks
Sea salt and milled black pepper
300g ripe tomatoes, roughly chopped
3 garlic cloves, finely sliced
1 handful fresh oregano, roughly chopped
200ml white wine

To serve
Roasted potatoes
Salad

1. Heat a heavy-based frying pan to medium high.

2. Smear some of the olive oil over the steaks, and season well with salt and pepper.

3. Place the steaks in the centre of the pan. Depending on their thickness, for medium rare, cook for 6 minutes, turning halfway through. For medium, allow 7-8 minutes, and for well done, allow 8-10 minutes.

4. Remove the steaks from the pan and keep warm.

5. Put the remaining olive oil in the pan, and add the tomatoes, garlic and oregano. Cook over a medium heat for a few minutes, then turn up the heat and add the white wine. Simmer the sauce for 3 minutes, until the volume reduces a little. Serve the steak with the sauce, roasted potatoes and a simple salad.

Fish

With more than its fair share of coastline, Italy is a wonderful place for lovers of fish and seafood. These recipes use simple, fresh flavours to create memorable dishes in minutes — whether you're looking for a midweek treat or something special for entertaining.

Sweet and Sour Sardines

Sweet and Sour Sardines

These sweet and sour flavours are common in southern Italy. They work beautifully with the rich, oily sardines. To make the recipe easier, ask your fishmonger to gut the fish and remove the bones for you.

Serves 4 10 mins preparation, 20 mins cooking

Ingredients
1kg fresh sardines, gutted and deboned
Oil for greasing the baking tray
75g stale breadcrumbs
25g pine nuts, toasted
25g raisins
2 salted anchovies, finely chopped
1 tablespoon white wine vinegar
1 bunch flat-leaf parsley, finely chopped
2 tablespoons extra virgin olive oil
1 lemon, cut into wedges

1. Pre-heat the oven to 200°C/fan 180°C/gas mark 6.

2. Place the sardines on a well-oiled baking tray, in a single layer.

3. In a bowl, mix together the breadcrumbs, pine nuts, raisins, anchovies, vinegar and parsley. Spoon this mixture into the cavity of each sardine – don't worry if bits fall out, as they'll cook nicely on the baking tray.

4. Drizzle the extra virgin olive oil over the sardines, and bake for 15-20 minutes until lightly golden and cooked through.

5. Serve with lemon wedges to squeeze over.

Griddled Tuna with Fennel, Lemon and Mint Salad

Griddled Tuna with Fennel, Lemon and Mint Salad

Seared fresh tuna is a luxurious treat. I love to serve it with this zesty fennel salad for an impressive lunch or supper.

Serves 4 10 mins preparation, 20 mins cooking

Ingredients
1 small red onion, halved and finely sliced
Juice of 1 lemon
4 x 150g tuna steaks
2 tablespoons olive oil
Sea salt and milled black pepper
1 fennel bulb, quartered, cored and finely
sliced (keep the feathery fronds, chopped)
½ bunch radishes, finely sliced
½ cucumber, halved lengthways, cored
and finely sliced
1 small bunch mint, finely chopped
1 small bunch flat-leaf parsley, finely chopped
25g rocket leaves

1. Place the red onion in a small bowl. Pour over half the lemon juice, and leave to stand for 10 minutes.

2. Heat a griddle pan until hot. Brush the tuna steaks with a little of the olive oil, and season on both sides with salt and plenty of pepper.

3. Place the tuna on the griddle pan and cook for 3-4 minutes on each side, until golden, charred and cooked, yet still pink in the middle. Keep to one side.

4. Place the sliced fennel, radishes, cucumber, mint and flat-leaf parsley in a large bowl, and toss together well. Add the rocket leaves, red onion and the rest of the lemon juice and olive oil. Mix the salad well, and divide between 4 serving plates.

5. Place the tuna steaks on top of the salad, and serve scattered with the chopped fennel fronds.

Chargrilled Squid with Radicchio and Raw Courgette Salad

Cooked quickly on a high heat, squid becomes surprisingly soft. Ask your fishmonger to clean and prepare it for you – then this recipe is as easy as it is tasty!

Serves 4 10 mins preparation, 10-15 mins cooking

Ingredients

4 medium squid, gutted, cleaned and skinned, with the tentacles separate from the main body
1 tablespoon olive oil
Sea salt and milled black pepper
1 pinch chilli flakes
2 small courgettes, green or yellow

2 tablespoons extra virgin olive oil
1 tablespoon red wine vinegar
1 head radicchio, finely shredded
1 small bunch dill, finely chopped
1 tablespoon capers, finely chopped

1. Heat a griddle pan until very hot.

2. Cut the main bodies of the squid along one side and flatten out. Cut a criss-cross pattern over the inside flesh and brush with a little olive oil. Season all the squid with a little salt and pepper, and a sprinkling of chilli flakes.

3. Place the tentacles on the griddle pan first. Then, after a minute, add the main bodies (criss-cross side down) and cook for 3 minutes on each side – be careful not to turn until they have charred griddle marks.

4. On a chopping board, slice the cooked squid into pieces.

5. Using a vegetable peeler, thinly slice the courgettes lengthways. Place these in a bowl.

6. Mix together the extra virgin olive oil and red wine vinegar, with a good pinch of salt and pepper. Pour this over the courgettes and toss well with the radicchio, dill and capers.

7. Spoon the salad onto serving plates, and place the cooked squid on top.
Serve immediately.

Chargrilled Squid with Radicchio and Raw Courgette Salad

Hake with Salsa Verde and Green Beans

Salsa verde is a great, fresh-tasting sauce to serve with all kinds of grilled and barbecued fish. Here we're using hake, which is a creamy, mild fish with a firm, meaty texture.

Serves 4 15-20 mins preparation, 10 mins cooking

Ingredients
4 x 150g hake fillet steaks, bone removed
Juice and grated zest of 1 lemon
Olive oil for frying

To serve
700g new potatoes
200g green beans

For the salsa verde
1 garlic clove, finely chopped
2 anchovy fillets, finely chopped
1 teaspoon capers, finely chopped
1 shallot, finely chopped
6 cornichons, finely chopped
1 handful flat-leaf parsley, finely chopped
1 handful mint or basil, finely chopped
50ml extra virgin olive oil
1 tablespoon sherry vinegar
Sea salt and milled black pepper

1. Tie a piece of kitchen string around the middle of the hake to hold together neatly for ease of cooking. Place the fish in a shallow dish. Sprinkle over the lemon juice and zest, and leave to stand while you prepare the salsa.

2. Place the garlic, anchovies, capers, shallot, cornichons and herbs in a bowl, and mix together well. Stir in the extra virgin olive oil and sherry vinegar, and season with salt and pepper to taste.

3. Remove the hake from the lemon juice, and pat dry with kitchen towel. Season with a little salt and pepper.

4. Heat a little olive oil in a frying pan, and cook the hake, flesh side down, for 3-4 minutes until golden. Turn the fish carefully, and cook the other side for a further 3-4 minutes.

5. Serve the hake with the salsa verde, boiled new potatoes and green beans.

Hake with Salsa Verde and Green Beans

Roasted Chilli-Stuffed Mussels

Roasted Chilli-Stuffed Mussels

With a slightly fiery, crispy breadcrumb topping, these mussels make a tasty change from 'moules marinière'. Served in half the shell, they're also much easier to eat.

Serves 2 10 mins preparation, 15 mins cooking

Ingredients

2 tablespoons olive oil
1 garlic clove, finely chopped
2 shallots, finely chopped
1 red chilli, finely chopped
2 anchovy fillets in olive oil, drained and finely chopped
50g white breadcrumbs

2 tablespoons flat-leaf parsley, finely chopped
Grated zest of 1 lemon
Sea salt and milled black pepper
1kg mussels, scrubbed and beards removed
150ml white wine
Extra virgin olive oil for drizzling

1. Heat the olive oil in a frying pan over a medium heat. Add the garlic, shallots and chilli, and cook for 3 minutes.

2. Add the anchovies, stirring until they've melted.

3. Lower the heat, and add the breadcrumbs. Cook until they've absorbed all the oil, and continue cooking for 2-3 minutes, stirring until they're lightly browned.

4. Stir in the parsley and lemon zest, and season with salt and pepper to taste. Keep the pan to one side.

5. Pre-heat the oven to 220°C/fan 200°C /gas mark 7.

6. Discard any of the cleaned mussels that are cracked or don't close when you tap them on the work surface.

7. Heat a large saucepan over a high heat. Add the mussels and a splash of white wine, cover and cook for 2-3 minutes. Shake the pan now and then, until the mussels start to open.

8. Drain the mussels in a colander, reserving the juice, and leave to cool slightly. Discard any that stay closed, then pull the remaining shells apart and discard the empty shell halves.

9. Lay the mussels, in their open shells, on a baking tray and spoon over the juices from the saucepan. Scatter with the breadcrumb mixture, and bake in the top of the oven for 2-3 minutes until lightly golden.

10. Serve the mussels in their shells, drizzled with extra virgin olive oil.

Contorni e Insalate
/ Sides and Salads

An imaginative side dish can make a huge difference to a main course, and doesn't take much more effort than preparing plain vegetables. Try these ideas for a change – they'll add a taste of Italy to all sorts of meat or fish dishes.

Deep-Fried Courgette Chips

Deep-Fried Courgette Chips

Light and crispy, these delicate chips really do melt in your mouth.

Serves 2 15 mins preparation, 5 mins cooking

Ingredients
250g courgettes
2 tablespoons plain flour
2 tablespoons cornflour
100ml ice-cold water
Vegetable oil for frying
2 tablespoons Parmesan cheese, finely grated
Milled black pepper

1. Slice the courgettes into thin 'chip' shapes, about 3mm x 7cm.

2. Place both flours in a bowl, and beat in 100ml of ice-cold water to make a smooth batter of pouring cream consistancy.

3. Half fill a medium saucepan with vegetable oil. Put on a high heat until it reaches 190°C. (To test the temperature, put a cube of bread in the pan. At 190°C, it will brown in 30 seconds.)

4. Drop a quarter of the courgette chips into the batter, turning to coat them. Lift them out with a slotted spoon or fish slice, and let the excess batter drip off.

5. Carefully lower the coated courgette pieces into the hot oil, and cook for 1-2 minutes until golden.

6. Remove them from the hot oil with a slotted spoon, and drain on kitchen paper. Sprinkle with Parmesan cheese and a good grinding of pepper.

7. Repeat with the remaining courgettes and serve immediately.

Crusted Aubergine Slices

The crunchy coating in this recipe is a lovely contrast to soft, creamy aubergine.

Serves 2 5 mins preparation, 8 mins cooking

Ingredients
2 large eggs
Sea salt and milled black pepper
150g polenta
25g Parmesan cheese, finely grated
25g plain flour
1 large aubergine, cut into 5mm slices
3 tablespoons olive oil

1. Break the eggs into a bowl, season with a little salt and pepper, and beat lightly.
2. Place the polenta, Parmesan and flour in a shallow dish.
3. Dip the aubergine slices in the egg, and then in the polenta mixture, pressing down well to coat.
4. Heat the olive oil in a large non-stick frying pan over a medium heat. Fry the aubergine slices for 2-3 minutes on each side, until golden brown.
5. Remove them from the pan with a spatula, and drain on kitchen paper.
   Serve immediately.

Crusted Aubergine Slices

Potato, Chard and Pecorino Bake

Potato, Chard and Pecorino Bake

A potato and veg dish in one, this creamy bake is especially good with roast chicken.

Serves 4 10 mins preparation, 20 mins cooking

Ingredients
350g chard
400g potatoes, peeled and thinly sliced
1 knob of butter
2 garlic cloves, finely sliced
Sea salt and milled black pepper
300ml double cream
75g Pecorino cheese, grated

1 litre ovenproof dish

1. Pre-heat the oven to 200°C/fan 180°C/gas mark 6.

2. Strip the chard leaves from the stalks, and keep to one side. Cut the stalks into sticks, about 6cm long.

3. Bring a pan of water to the boil, and cook the potatoes for 4 minutes. Then add the chard sticks, and cook for 1 minute more. Add the leaves, cook for another minute, just until they've wilted. Drain and keep to one side.

4. Heat the butter in a small, 1 litre ovenproof dish. Add the garlic and cook for a minute, until it turns a light golden colour.

5. Add the chard sticks, leaves and potatoes, tossing well with the garlic, season with salt and pepper.

6. Pour the double cream over, and scatter with grated Pecorino. Bake for 15 minutes, until bubbling and golden, and serve straight from the dish.

Panzanella Salad

This is a great summer salad, packed with Mediterranean flavours – and a fun way to use up stale bread.

Serves 4 10 mins preparation, 5 mins cooking

Ingredients
150g good stale bread, about 2-3 days old, diced
2 tablespoons of olive oil
1 small cucumber, roughly chopped
1 red onion, roughly chopped
6 ripe tomatoes, roughly chopped
Sea salt and milled black pepper
3 tablespoons extra virgin olive oil
2 tablespoons red wine vinegar
2 tablespoons capers, chopped
1 handful basil leaves, roughly torn

1. Pre-heat the oven to 200°C/fan 180°C/gas mark 6. Place the diced bread on a baking tray and drizzle over the olive oil. Toss together well and bake for 5-7 minutes until golden and crusty.

2. Place the cucumber, red onion and tomatoes in a large bowl, and add the toasted bread. Mix well with your hands, and season to taste with salt and pepper.

3. Whisk the extra virgin olive oil, red wine vinegar and capers with a good grinding of pepper. Pour this over the salad, and toss together well. Finally, scatter the basil leaves on top.

Panzanella Salad

Dolce / Desserts

Rounding off an Italian meal usually involves something quite light but very indulgent. So most of these recipes feature fresh fruit, along with luxuriously rich ingredients, such as mascarpone or Marsala wine – and I haven't forgotten something for chocolate lovers.

Strawberries with Balsamic Syrup and Mascarpone Cream

Strawberries with Balsamic Syrup and Mascarpone Cream

Balsamic vinegar really enhances the flavour of strawberries, especially when made into a sweet syrup. And with my creamy mascarpone topping, you have the perfect summer dessert.

Serves 4 10 mins preparation, 5 mins cooking

Ingredients
300g strawberries
50g caster sugar
4 tablespoons balsamic vinegar
150ml whipping cream
150g mascarpone
2 tablespoons icing sugar
1 small handful basil leaves

1. Hull the strawberries (remove the green top and core). Slice and place in a large bowl.

2. Place the sugar and balsamic vinegar in a small saucepan over a medium heat, and bring to a gentle simmer. Cook for 5 minutes, until the volume reduces by half.

3. Whip the cream, mascarpone and icing sugar together, until you have a thick, creamy, spoonable mixture.

4. Spoon the strawberries into serving bowls. Drizzle over the balsamic syrup, and top with a spoonful of mascarpone cream and a few basil leaves.

Peach and Prosecco Sorbet

Peach and Prosecco Sorbet

This semi-frozen dessert is a really refreshing way to round off a meal – especially in the summer when fresh peaches are at their best.

Serves 4 5 mins preparation, 4-5 hours freezing

Ingredients
400g fresh ripe peaches (about 4)
or 400g tinned peaches, drained,
plus extra for serving
Juice and grated zest of 1 lemon
200ml Prosecco
50g caster sugar

Food processor

1. Place the peaches in a food processor with the lemon zest and juice, Prosecco and sugar, and blend until smooth.
2. Pour the mixture into a shallow dish, and freeze for 4-5 hours until firm.
3. With an ice cream scoop, scoop the mixture into balls and serve with chunks of fresh peach.

Zabaglione with Amaretti Crumbs

Zabaglione is a luxurious dessert consisting of whipped and heated egg yolks, sugar and Marsala wine. The secret is to whisk it for long enough to take lots of air into the mixture. That way, you end up with a light texture – in contrast to the indulgently rich flavour.

Serves 4   20 mins preparation

Ingredients
75g amaretti biscuits
6 large egg yolks
1 vanilla pod, split lengthways
150g caster sugar
100ml dry Marsala wine

Food processor
Electric whisk

1. Place the amaretti biscuits in a food processor, and blitz until you have coarse crumbs. (Or put them in a plastic bag, seal, and crush using a rolling pin.)

2. Put the egg yolks in a large bowl, over a pan of just-simmering water.

3. Using a sharp knife, scrape the seeds from the vanilla pod into the eggs, and then add the sugar.

4. Using an electric whisk, beat the yolks, vanilla and sugar for about 15 minutes, until the mixture is pale, thick and fluffy.

5. Gradually whisk in the Marsala, and then remove the bowl from the pan of water. Continue to whisk until the zabaglione has cooled slightly. Leave it to cool further and thicken for 5 minutes.

6. Divide the mixture between 4 serving glasses, and sprinkle with a layer of the amaretti crumbs.

Zabaglione with Amaretti Crumbs

Baked Pears with Chocolate Sauce

Of all the ways of combining pears with chocolate, this is my favourite. Adding vanilla gives extra depth of flavour, and the simple chocolate sauce is totally irresistible!

Serves 4 10 mins preparation, 20 mins cooking

Ingredients
75g caster sugar
1 vanilla pod, split lengthways
6 ripe small pears, peeled, halved and cored
Juice of 1 lemon
2 tablespoons water
25g unsalted butter, diced
100g dark chocolate, roughly chopped
300ml double cream

To serve
75g torrone (Italian nougat), roughly chopped

Large baking dish

1. Pre-heat the oven to 200°C/fan 180°C/gas mark 6.
2. Place the sugar in a bowl. With a sharp knife, scrape the seeds from the vanilla pod, and stir into the sugar. Keep the vanilla pod.
3. Arrange the pears in a large baking dish, cut side up. Drizzle the lemon juice evenly over the fruit, and then sprinkle with the vanilla sugar.
4. Cut the vanilla pod you've saved into quarters, and place these among the pear halves. Pour the water into the dish, then dot each pear with butter.
5. Place the dish in the oven and bake for 10 minutes. Then turn the pears over, and continue cooking for a further 10 minutes.
6. Meanwhile, place the chocolate and cream in a saucepan. Heat gently, until the chocolate melts and you have a smooth, creamy sauce.
7. Serve the pear halves alongside the chocolate sauce and chopped torrone.

Baked Pears with Chocolate Sauce

Baked Golden Nectarines with Almonds and Marsala

Baked Golden Nectarines with Almonds and Marsala

The flavour of almonds works beautifully with the sweetness of nectarines – so this crunchy amaretti and almond topping always goes down well.

Serves 4 10 mins preparation, 20 mins cooking

Ingredients
4 ripe nectarines, halved and the stones removed
100g amaretti biscuits
100g butter, softened
60g ground almonds
60g caster sugar
1 medium egg
2 tablespoons flaked almonds
150ml dry Marsala wine

Food processor

To serve
Vanilla ice cream

1. Pre-heat the oven to 200°C/fan 180°C/gas mark 6.

2. Arrange the nectarines in a single layer in a shallow roasting tin, cut side up.

3. Place the amaretti in a food processor, and blitz until you have coarse crumbs. (Or put them in a plastic bag, seal, and crush them using a rolling pin.)

4. Put the crumbs in a bowl, and add the butter, ground almonds, sugar and egg, mix well.

5. Spoon the mixture into the cavities of the nectarines, and scatter the flaked almonds over the top. Pour the Marsala into the bottom of the tin, and bake for 20 minutes until the topping and filling are golden and crunchy, and the nectarines are tender.

6. Serve warm with the juices spooned over, and scoops of vanilla ice cream.

Bevande / Drinks

As the home of Martini, Campari, Aperol and Prosecco, Italy has produced many classic aperitifs and cocktails. I've included three of my favourites here – all designed to get any occasion off to a stylish, celebratory start.

Bellini

Invented at Harry's Bar in Venice in the 1930s, this famous cocktail is still very popular as a celebration drink. Try it with thin torinesi bread sticks or quartered ripe figs wrapped in Parma ham.

Serves 4 10 mins preparation

Ingredients
2 ripe peaches or 4 tinned peach halves
in natural juice, including skins
Chilled Champagne or dry Prosecco

Blender

1. Place the peaches in a blender and whiz until they're really smooth.

2. Spoon a few teaspoons of the peach purée into each of 4 Champagne glasses.

3. Gently pour in the Champagne or Prosecco, stirring as you go, and serve straight away.

Negroni

Reputedly invented in Florence in the early 20th century, this classic aperitif cocktail combines the semi-sweetness of Martini Rosso with the distinctive bitter taste of Campari. And with a good slug of gin, you probably need only one!

Serves 1 5 mins preparation

Ingredients
Ice cubes
1 orange, sliced
30ml Martini Rosso

30ml Campari
30ml gin

1. Fill a jug with ice cubes and orange slices. Add the Martini, Campari and gin, and mix well.

2. Pour into tumblers and serve.

Aperol Spritz

Aperol Spritz

Similar in taste to Campari, but lower in alcohol, Aperol makes a refreshing aperitif –
especially when you liven it up with Prosecco.

Serves 1 5 mins preparation

Ingredients
Ice cubes
60ml Aperol
100ml Prosecco

Splash of soda water
Slices of lime

1. Place lots of ice in a tall glass.

2. Pour the Aperol over the ice, and then add the Prosecco.

3. Stir gently, top with soda water and add a few slices of lime.

About Howdens Joinery

The Italian kitchen is the perfect place for anyone who loves to cook, combining great design and functionality. The kitchen shown and a number of the products featured are produced in Italy and take inspiration from Italian design.

Howdens Joinery offers a range of integrated kitchen, appliance and joinery products designed to meet the needs of modern living.

Our offer includes over 40 different kitchen designs, plus a full range of accessories, worktops, doors, flooring, skirting, and a wide variety of Lamona appliances, sinks and taps, exclusive to Howdens. The Lamona range has been selected to perfectly complement our range of kitchens, and products are manufactured to the highest standards to ensure they are durable and reliable.

Last year we supplied over 350,000 kitchens, 600,000 appliances and 550,000 sinks and taps to UK homes.

To find out more or locate one of over 550 nationwide depots, visit **www.howdens.com**

Internal Soft Close 3 Drawer Base Unit

Gloss White and Graphite Integrated Handle Kitchen

1400rpm Integrated Washer Dryer

Lamona Front Touch Control Ceramic Hob

Lamona Windermere Single Bowl Sink with Lamona Chrome
Cubic Single Lever Tap

About the author

Food writer and home economist Angela Boggiano was born in England to parents from Liguria in northern Italy. She grew up learning tried and trusted family recipes, and went on to work with leading chefs such as Giorgio Locatelli, Gennaro Contaldo and Valentina Harris.

Angela has edited various food publications and this is just one of several Italian cookbooks that she has contributed to, including "The Italian Kitchen" and "Recipes from my Italian Grandmother". This latest collaboration demonstrates the wonderful wealth of flavours the country has to offer.

Exclusive to Howdens Joinery Co.

www.lamona.co.uk